SMART

Ways for Learning

SPANISH

María Blanco MA, FHEA

This is a work of nonfiction. Names and identifying details have been changed.

Copyright ©2017 by María Teresa Blanco Hermida

All rights reserved. No part of this publication may be copied, stored, reproduced, distributed or transmitted using any form and by any means including photocopying, electronic devices, computers of any kind including mobile phones without the explicit and prior written permission of the author, except in the case of brief quotations for reviews.

Cover design by Nina Dedeken

Published by María Teresa Blanco Hermida

Printed by Createspace, an Amazon Company

To Ratu Bagus and my parents

Contents

1 ▶ Introduction 7

2 ▶ What motivates you? 9

3 ▶ Good language learners 17

4 ▶ Two complementary approaches 22

5 ▶ Get focused and energized 24

6 ▶ Interesting and comprehensible 31

7 ▶ Four good friends 35

8 ▶ The key ingredients of speaking 42

9 ▶ The whys and hows of learning vocabulary ... 45

10 ▶ Strategies for pronunciation 56

11 ▶ Are you enthusiastic about grammar? 65

12 ▶ Automatizing grammar 70

13 ▶ Flashcards 74

14 ▶ A materials kit 81

15 ▶ Good courses and teachers 85

16 ▶ Deep diving 90

17 ▶ More immersion options 96

18 ▶ On ceilings 102

5

19 ▶ What to do next?..110
20 ▶ Acknowledgements..113
21 ▶ About the author..116
22 ▶ Resources..119

1 ▶ Introduction

The idea for writing "SMART Ways for Learning Spanish" came to me years ago, while I was teaching Spanish as a Foreign Language to groups of adults in the UK. The students were highly motivated and participated well in the class activities in spite of having little previous experience of learning foreign languages at school, but they were rather lost as to how to study the language by themselves outside the class. From time to time, some of them would ask me for tips for further improving their Spanish pronunciation or grammar when studying at home. I noticed they were receptive and very appreciative of any suggestions I gave on smart strategies.

As time went by, I realized that, just like me, most students I was teaching had no training in effective strategies for learning foreign languages by themselves. For example, even intermediate level students often learned new words and phrases only by repeating them out loud or by writing them out several times. Very few of them regularly used strategies proven to be more effective for long-term retention of vocabulary, such as multisensory associations, flashcards, or mind maps. I also found many beginners unaware of simple techniques that could be used from day one to develop good Spanish speaking and listening skills.

So, little by little, after becoming convinced that writing a book on simple and effective how-to-learn strategies could help many students, I started researching the topic and including more discussions on **smart strategies** in my Spanish lessons. The overall results have been, and remain, very positive. I find that students who regularly apply the smart strategies I discuss in this book speed up their learning, improve their exam results, become more self-confident, and, most importantly, experience more enjoyment as they learn. And the good news is that it is simple to put the strategies into practice. So, let's discuss them!

2 ▶ What motivates you?

It was the first day of the Spanish beginners' class and I invited the students to share with the group their reasons for taking the course. Sue was the first to speak: "Dave and I are retiring next year and are planning to move to the flat we have in Santa Pola, near Alicante. We've been holidaying there for a long time. We love the sea and the climate, and we have nice Spanish neighbors. The only problem so far is that they hardly speak any English and we hardly speak any Spanish. Our conversations are rather short at the moment! We're also planning to travel through Spain, to see different places and get to know more about the culture. Learning some Spanish will be handy for all that." Dave nodded in agreement.

John spoke next. "Unfortunately, retirement is still far away for me and Daisy, but we've just started building a house on the outskirts of Alicante, not far from Santa Pola. We've also been going on holiday to this part of the country for many years and have made some very good friends at the sailing club. We'd like to speak better Spanish to mix more with the locals and socialize more." Daisy added, "What John is not telling you is that he also wants to check on the Spanish builders!" Everyone in the class laughed.

They were a delightful group of adult students. They were focused during the lessons, got on well, and had a shared sense of humor. The atmosphere in class was positive during the first weeks of the course. But after a while, things changed. Sue, David, John, and Daisy were lagging behind the rest of the group and looking rather stressed about it. I tried to encourage them to focus on their own progress instead of constantly comparing themselves with other students, but they did not seem persuaded. Around mid-November, both couples said they were finding the course much harder than expected. They insisted that everybody else seemed to be doing better than them, and talked about the possibility of dropping the course.

Then one day, at the end of the lesson, the four of them approached my desk. John took the lead and said, "María, just to let you know that Daisy and I have decided not to give up the Spanish course just yet. I'm not sure whether I'll ever be able to show off my Spanish at the sailing club but I definitely want to check on the builders." We all chuckled. Then Sue spoke. "Dave and I are sticking to the course too. The grammar is hard, but we're just going to get on with it. We want to be able to chat with our Spanish neighbors and friends in Santa Pola."

Fortunately, both couples carried on attending the lessons. None of them were amongst the best in the class but by the end of the year they had learned a lot and gained a great deal of confidence in their ability to learn Spanish. It was a great experience to see how much progress they had made and to play a part in the happy ending.

During the summer holidays, after the course had finished, I got postcards from them. Both couples were in Alicante again, trying out their much improved Spanish with their neighbors and friends. They were having a more satisfying social life. Daisy also mentioned how the builders were behaving better since they realized that John could understand and speak more Spanish.

The story of Sue, David, John, and Daisy is similar to the story of many other students I have taught. Strong motivation gets them through the challenges and sustains their drive to achieve better communication skills in Spanish. There is also the bonus of feeling more confident about their ability to learn a new language.

The other students in that same beginners' class were motivated to learn Spanish for a wide variety of reasons. Laura was preparing for her trip to Santiago de Chile; she was meeting her boyfriend's family and friends and was keen to connect with them and the culture through their mother tongue. Maggie and Harry just wanted to learn something new and do something different than what they did in their daytime jobs. Marc loved languages and wanted to enhance his career prospects by adding Spanish to his CV. Dorinne was planning to move with her husband and two children to a small village in the south east of Spain to set up an organic farm. And then there was Hanna, who took the course simply because she loved the sound of the Spanish language.

What about you? What motivates you to learn Spanish? Think about it for a moment. Understanding your own **motivation** will help you activate the inner and outer resources you need to make good progress and to enjoy more the whole process of learning. Clarity about your motivation will also give you meaning, and the energy to break through some of the challenges that will come along as you learn Spanish.

Do any of the following statements reflect your motivation? If not, how would you describe what motivates you?

▶ I want to travel to Spanish speaking countries.

▶ I want to move to and live in Spanish speaking countries.

▶ I want to be more integrated in the Spanish speaking country where I live.

▶ I want to connect more with people from Spanish speaking countries.

▶ I want to use Spanish in my job, with my customers.

▶ I want to explore Hispanic culture (cinema, literature, art) in more depth.

▶ I love the way the Spanish language sounds.

▶ I love learning languages.

▶ I want to develop a new skill.

▶ I want to learn something new.

Spanish, a worldwide language
Did you know?

▶ Spanish is an official language in 21 countries: *México, Colombia, Spain, Argentina, Peru, Venezuela, Chile, Guatemala, Ecuador, Cuba, Bolivia, República Dominicana, Honduras, Paraguay, El Salvador, Nicaragua, Costa Rica, Panamá, Puerto Rico, Uruguay,* and *Guinea Ecuatorial.*

▶ There are more than 56 million Spanish speakers in the United States.

▶ Nearly 570 million people across the world speak Spanish, and the Instituto Cervantes predicts that the number will increase to 754 million by 2050.

▶ Spanish is currently the third most widely used language on the internet, and the second most widely used on Facebook and Twitter.

▶ Worldwide, more than 21 million students study Spanish as a Foreign Language.

El español: una lengua viva (2016)

Instituto Cervantes

3 ▶ Good language learners

I met Susie on the first day of a one-week teacher training course in Madrid. Very soon after we had been introduced, I noticed she was keen on practicing her basic Spanish with me and other Spanish native speakers attending the training. On one of the occasions we were chatting, she was struggling to tell me something in Spanish and I asked whether she would prefer us to switch to English. She responded without hesitation, "No, gracias. Prefiero hablar español. Necesito practicar," which means, "No, thank you. I prefer to speak in Spanish. I need to practice."

As the days went by, I became more impressed with Susie's skilful way of communicating in Spanish with such a small repertoire of vocabulary. I asked her, "How have you been learning Spanish so far? Have you done a course?"

"Kind of... I've studied mostly by myself, with the help of good online materials. I love taking language courses but I haven't managed to do a Spanish course yet. Right now, I'm busy managing new projects at work and busy with my children at home. There's not much point in enrolling in a course at the moment. Instead, I'm studying by myself, at my own pace, using the Spanish online materials from the Instituto Cervantes."

"And is that the only formal studying you've done?"

"Yes! And our lunchtime chat on the first day we met was my first serious attempt at having a real-life conversation with a native speaker of Spanish – although I confess that I've learned some Italian before. Both languages are fairly similar, and that helps a lot."

Susie and I got on well and spent a lot of time together during that week. I could see her moving around and taking full advantage of opportunities to mingle with Spanish native speakers. Several times on sightseeing tours, I spotted her joining the

Spanish tourist guide instead of the English one, checking her dictionary and switching from Spanish to English to ask some of her friends for translations of what the guide was saying. She was determined but also playful and patient with herself while practicing the language; it was fascinating to see how she was making the best of that immersion situation for practicing Spanish. Susie remains one of the most proactive Spanish language students I have ever met.

What makes some people, like Susie, do so well at learning foreign languages? This question started to interest me many years ago. I began to pay more attention to the attitudes and skills displayed by students who seemed to learn Spanish easily. Also, while taking my MA in Modern Languages, I read a good number of research studies that investigated what makes some students good language learners. The studies found that people who are good at languages use a wide range of language learning strategies, and are particularly skillful at using key **self-management strategies** such as planning, checking progress, problem-solving, and self-assessment. Researchers have also found that good language learners:

▶ are able to maintain a good level of motivation because they have many reasons to learn

▶ take an active approach to learning

▶ develop strategies appropriate to their individual needs

▶ analyze how language works

▶ pay attention to the meaning and form of words

▶ seek opportunities to practice the language in real-life situations

▶ take some risks in communication

▶ adapt to different learning environments.

I was not surprised by these conclusions since they are all very much in tune with what I notice in the behavior of students who learn Spanish and other foreign languages easily.

What about you? What has helped you succeed when learning foreign languages? Have you used similar strategies to the ones just mentioned? Which ones? And are there any other smart strategies that you use and that could help you learn Spanish effectively now?

Remember that success leaves footprints. If you pay attention to what has helped your own success and other people's, you will get inspiration, insights, and valuable tools for building a more positive learning experience.

4 ▶ Two complementary approaches

There are two complementary approaches to learning Spanish. One is the classic, **formal** approach that most of us have experienced at school. This approach involves activities such as: joining a Spanish language course or getting a private tutor; scheduling self-study time; practicing vocabulary, grammar, and pronunciation with the support of educational materials, and so on. The second approach is **informal.** It involves immersing yourself in environments where you get to use Spanish as "naturally" as possible without thinking too much about how the language works. Typical informal learning activities are: listening to Spanish music, watching movies, playing computer games, interacting with native speakers through social media, and taking advantage of any opportunities that arise for practicing the language with native speakers.

In my experience, the combination of the two approaches, formal and informal, is powerful because each one fulfills different and vital language learning needs. After many years of teaching, I have no doubt that students who want to become both fluent and precise in Spanish need formal and informal language learning activities. The combination is highly effective and makes learning more enjoyable. We discuss both approaches in more detail in the coming chapters.

5 ▶ Get focused and energized

My first attempt at setting **goals** for learning English was not very successful. I did it a long time ago, when goal setting was becoming fashionable in career development workshops. At that time, I had not read or heard anybody talk about goal setting for language learning, but I thought it could be useful for my self-study in English and decided to give it a try.

Setting goals was largely guesswork since I did not have access to any specific examples and did not know of anybody who had experience in this. Nevertheless, I gave it a try. I wrote down a short list of goals and started working towards them. But the process was unpleasant. The specific outcomes and time frames that I had set for myself were making me more anxious, and I noticed that they were slowing down my learning instead of speeding it up. I tried to modify the goals but it did not seem to make much of a difference, and I gave up after a few attempts.

Years later, while taking a course in coaching and management skills, I decided to give goal setting another try. This time, the situation was different. First of all, I had had more training in setting goals and was more familiar with the process. Secondly, I was ready to take a more creative approach and was more relaxed about experimenting with the process. After reflecting on what had not worked previously, I decided to set a general goal that was thrilling for me and to take a more flexible approach to the time frames of the tasks I needed to do to achieve the goal. My general goal was: "to improve my English pronunciation so that I can be easily understood by international audiences". And I committed to spending a minimum of two hours a week doing the following:

▶ completing activities from a pronunciation workbook and software

▶ listening to and singing along with my favorite English songs

▶ practicing speech shadowing with BBC video and audio clips.

The results of my goal setting activity were very different this time. I was focused and energized, and I had more fun while practicing my English pronunciation, both formally and informally. I also noticed improvements in my pronunciation, and people around me started complimenting me on the changes.

I often meet students who experience similar difficulties to the ones I had the first time I experimented with goal setting. They do not set goals that are truly exciting for them, and/or they set goals that are too ambitious for the time and resources they have available at a particular point in time. Overall, I find that most of us need some guidance when it comes to setting learning goals because we rarely get to develop this skill during our formal education. And one simple way of getting some guidance is reading language learning goals such as the following examples:

Communicative goals

▶ get by in Spanish: greet friends and say goodbye, order food and drinks, go shopping, and so on

▶ discuss current world affairs with native speakers

▶ understand the news on TV and in the newspapers without constantly having to resort to the dictionary

▶ negotiate a business contract

Proficiency level goals

▶ achieve a "get by"/intermediate /advanced level

▶ maintain my current level of Spanish

▶ get an international certificate in Spanish as a Foreign Language such as DELE or SIELE

Other goals

▶ design flashcards with vocabulary from topics covered in my Spanish lessons

▶ learn specific vocabulary for writing emails and dealing with phone calls

- ▶ get into the habit of checking the meaning, and listening to and repeating the
    pronunciation of words I want to learn
- ▶ correct some of the recurrent errors I make in pronunciation
- ▶ discuss films and books more fluently
- ▶ improve my capacity to ask questions
- ▶ memorize verb endings of the present subjunctive tense
- ▶ spend 30 minutes four days a week working through my self-study pack.

Let's now explore your goals. What Spanish learning goals energize you right now? What do you find energizing about the goals? Are you already clear? If you are, write down the goals, read them out loud, and see whether they resonate with what you really want and are ready to work for at this point in time. If you are not clear yet, you could explore some of the following goal setting strategies:

▶ Link your Spanish learning goals to a dream you have, as I did and still do with English pronunciation. One of my dreams is to give talks to and lead workshops with international audiences on smart learning strategies for Spanish. Linking my pronunciation work to the dream helps me to focus and enjoy more the process of practicing.

▶ Start your goals with action words such as "increase", "maintain", "correct", "complete".

▶ Engage your imagination and senses. Imagine you have already achieved the goals. Where do you see yourself? What are you doing? What can you hear? What can you feel? Draw a picture and/or describe to yourself or somebody else what you have just seen, heard, and felt.

▶ Ask a coach or teacher to help you gain clarity about your goals.

Once you have set your goals, the next two questions are: How are you going to achieve the goal(s) you have set? What kind of time frame are you going to set? I do not think there are fixed formulas that work for everybody when it comes to how to achieve learning goals and what time frames to set. The ways and times vary according to the individual. For example, I have noticed that some students I coach get more focused and energized by tight goal deadlines while other students freeze up. So I suggest that you explore and fine tune the process until you find the kind of goals, tasks, and time frames that work best for you.

6 ▶ Interesting and comprehensible

I was taken aback by Alice's request when she approached me during the break of our first Spanish advanced level class.

"Could I please have a reading list of Spanish books?"

"Yes. There's a list available on our Spanish website. What kind of books do you like reading?"

"All sorts, but mainly science fiction, stories of intrigue. Anything with a good plot."

"Have you read any Spanish books?"

"I haven't, but I sometimes read newspapers and magazines. I'd like to try books now."

What took me aback me about Alice's request was her being so proactive. She had not even waited until the end of the first class!

Alice's spoken Spanish was not particularly good at the start of the course, taking into account that she had studied Spanish for several years at school. Many other students in the class spoke more fluently and displayed a more sophisticated range of vocabulary. But the situation started shifting about three months later. I noticed Alice's language skills were getting better with each class, and by the end of the year she was one of the best in the group.

In the final exam, Alice's oral presentation was by far the best in the class, and the best I had seen for many years at advanced level. She used specialist vocabulary very well, her grammar was refined, and there was a great deal of poise in her delivery. The rest of the group looked impressed. They all went quiet and listened to her presentation with a great deal of attention.

A couple of days later, before traveling back to her hometown in France, she came to my office to say goodbye.

"Thanks for the classes, Maria. I very much enjoyed your Spanish lessons."

"I'm glad. I enjoyed teaching you too. It was a pleasure to see you making so much progress during the year, and even more to see the outstanding quality of your presentation. How did you do it?"

"Well, reading a lot in Spanish made a big difference for me this year. Apart from the usual newspapers, I managed to read four books on the course reading list – books by Isabel Allende and Manuel Vazquez Montalbán. I loved the books and got more confident. I realized that I could understand a lot more than I expected. I felt great. I also watched a few of the Almodóvar films from the library. My housemate is studying Spanish so we watched them together. I use subtitles because some of the characters speak very fast but I enjoy watching Almodóvar´s films very much. And the more I watch, the easier it gets."

Alice's story illustrates a powerful principle at work: reading and listening regularly to Spanish which is **interesting and comprehensible** is one of the smartest things you can do for learning the language with ease. When the content is interesting and you can understand most of it, you become motivated to keep reading and listening, and you pay more attention to the language. The more attention you pay and the more you understand, the more language "sticks" in your memory. The more language sticks in your memory, the more it expands your ability to understand and express yourself. It is a virtuous circle of success, just as happened to Alice.

Are you applying this principle right now? If not, are there any interesting and comprehensible Spanish materials you could use? Could you borrow or buy some? It is a good investment of time and money – you will get good returns.

You can find suggestions for materials on my website: www.smartlearningforspanish.com.

7 ▶ Four good friends

Have you noticed the strong connection between listening and speaking skills when it comes to foreign language learning? And have you realized that you need to do a fair amount of listening to be good at speaking? Through listening, we get to hear the sounds that we need to imitate in speaking, and to hear examples of how vocabulary is used in the spoken language. Knowing how to pronounce Spanish well and how to use the language in spoken interaction is essential if you want to be good at speaking. Good listening skills are also essential if you want to be able to participate in formal and informal conversations with Spanish speakers.

Other language skills are strongly interconnected as well. For example, as I mentioned in the previous chapter, reading gives you exposure to a wide range of vocabulary and grammar structures. And as your range of vocabulary and grammar increases, so in turn does your ability to understand through listening and reading and your ability to express yourself through speaking or writing.

Writing supports good speaking too. When writing, you usually have time to: reflect on how best to say what you want to say, think about appropriate vocabulary and grammar, check the dictionary, review word order, and edit the message you are trying to convey. Writing is good preparation for good quality speaking – I have no doubt about this. I have seen it happen many times with my students: they speak better Spanish once they have practiced writing on the topic they are going to talk about, and the quality of their speaking is even better if, in addition to writing, they have done intensive reading and listening on the topic.

So this is another powerful language learning principle to take into consideration: **listening**, **reading**, **speaking**, and **writing** are "good friends".

They are strongly connected, and support each other as good friends do.

Experiencing gaps

There was a quiet knock on my office door. A student I did not recognize opened the door.

"Hi. My name is Yana. I'm struggling a bit with my Spanish course and my teacher said that you may be able to help with learning strategies."

"OK, let's talk about it. Have a seat… What are you struggling with?"

"I'm finding the speaking part hard. The problem is that I can understand a lot more than I can say. I had the same problem when I did Spanish at school, and it's the same when I go on holiday with my family to southern Spain."

Sometimes I come across students who, like Yana, are worried that they understand a lot more than what they are able to say or write in Spanish. They often think that it is due to not being good at speaking and writing but that is usually not the case.

The gap between receptive language skills (reading and listening) and productive language skills (writing and speaking) is natural. If you think about it, you will notice that we have the same experience in our mother tongue. We may easily understand the speeches of highly articulate public speakers, but, for most of us, it is not easy to write or deliver similar speeches. And the same goes for writing: understanding Mario Vargas Llosa novels without a problem does not mean that we can easily write literary works like his.

The gap between receptive and productive language skills often widens when people listen to native speakers and read a lot while traveling in Spanish speaking countries. They often read a lot of signs, timetables, and tourist brochures, and they listen to conversations, and so on. But they avoid or simply manage to get by without having to speak or write much during their trip. The bottom line is that, albeit unconsciously, they have practiced reading and listening skills a lot more than speaking and writing. Hence, the increase in the gap.

Some language teaching methods can also widen the gaps between skills. For example, my English schoolteachers spent most of the time teaching us grammar and vocabulary and practicing reading skills. We hardly did any listening and speaking practice in the lessons. So on my first trips to the UK, I managed to understand things like museum brochures and menus but I could not understand native speakers at all when they spoke to me, not even when they used the most basic words and phrases such as prices or phone numbers. Speaking was even harder: I could not even introduce myself and say, "My name is Maria" without blushing! My speaking and listening skills were basically zero at that time but I was reasonably comfortable reading and writing in real-life situations. The gap was so big that I thought I would never manage to get my speaking and listening up to speed. Fortunately, time showed otherwise.

Children who are brought up speaking Spanish at home but are living in a non-Spanish speaking country like the UK tend to experience the opposite of what I did at school. They develop strong listening and speaking skills because that is how they communicate with their parents at home from childhood. They are brought up on a diet of intensive listening and speaking, but are hardly ever put into a situation where they need to write or understand a written text. So when they grow up, it is easy for them to speak fluently but many of them cannot write without making a lot of spelling errors.

There is nothing wrong with experiencing different levels of proficiency in different language skills. Not at all. The situation only becomes problematic if you are finding that the gap between skills prevents you from communicating in the way you need or want to communicate with others. If that is the case, it is time for action. It is time to take a course, find a tutor, and increase informal practice or any other language learning activity that can help you to improve your ability in the language skills that are less developed.

8 ▶ The key ingredients of speaking

Julia was looking upset after her Spanish oral exam. "My speaking isn't good," she said before leaving the classroom. Unfortunately, we did not have time to talk. I was pressed for time – the next student to be examined was already waiting at the door.

I kept thinking about Julia's comment after the exam. Her pronunciation was excellent, probably one of the best in the class, and her range of vocabulary was good. The weak points in her speaking were grammar and fluency. She was quite slow and hesitant, and made mistakes when using verbs and sentences with noun and adjective agreements.

I have seen similar processes taking place with other students when they do a spoken performance: the lack of good grammar skills slows down fluency, self-doubt kicks in, and they conclude that they are not good at speaking. But, as in Julia's case, their conclusion is an overgeneralization. The problem is not their speaking skill as a whole. The weakness, and what needs to be improved, is often one of the key ingredients of the spoken language, which in Julia's case was grammar.

Andy's speaking was different to Julia's. He was a highly motivated student, able to use a very good range of vocabulary and grammar in speaking, but experiencing difficulties with pronunciation. Some of the sounds of Spanish were new to him; they did not exist in his mother tongue. Andy's writing was excellent but his spoken Spanish was hard to understand. The solution for him was to work more on pronunciation, another key ingredient of the spoken language.

From time to time, I also find students whose biggest limitation for speaking is the small repertoire of vocabulary they have. But this weakness is rather unusual. It is more common to find students who need to boost their pronunciation and grammar in order to get their speaking skills up to a satisfactory level.

So remember: to speak fluently and with a good degree of precision you need to develop all three key ingredients of the spoken language. The number one key ingredient is **vocabulary**: we can't communicate at all without vocabulary. The number two key ingredient is **pronunciation**: we need to pronounce vocabulary reasonably well if we want to be understood. And **grammar** is the key ingredient number three: a good command of grammar rules and structures helps us to understand and express ideas with accuracy. It's the icing on the cake!

What about your speaking skills? How are you doing with the key ingredients? Is there any particular one that needs more attention?

9 ▶ The whys and hows of learning vocabulary

"The fact is that without grammar very little can be conveyed; without vocabulary nothing at all can be conveyed." D. Wilkins

I guess you do not need persuading about the importance of learning a good range of Spanish words and phrases on a variety of topics. As the British linguist Wilkins succinctly puts it, without vocabulary nothing can be conveyed.

There are two basic approaches that you can take to learning vocabulary. The first is **learning by exposure**. This approach involves learning words and phrases by being exposed to them over and over again through reading and listening. Through exposure, you become familiar with the meaning, spelling, and pronunciation of words and phrases, as well as with the different ways in which the words and phrases can be used. The second approach is the **intentional study** of vocabulary. Intentional study involves focusing on committing to memory specific words and phrases through the use of techniques such as flashcards, vocabulary notebooks, or mind maps.

Both approaches have their advantages and their limitations, and, in my experience, a combination of both is what produces the best results. Combining learning by exposure with intentional study of specific words and phrases helps to enliven the experience of learning new words and improves long-term memorization.

What vocabulary are you going to learn?

I suggest you prioritize the following four categories – they will expand your ability to communicate in a short period of time:

▶ **Cognates.** These are Spanish words that are similar or identical, in meaning and spelling, to words you already know in other languages. For example, speakers of English would find it easy to learn cognates such as *aeropuerto*, *restaurante*, *cámara*, *hotel*, and *teléfono*. But when learning cognates, you also need to remember that there are a small number of "false cognates": that is, words with identical or similar spelling which mean something slightly, or even completely, different. Examples are: *arena* (sand), *carpeta* (folder), and *sensible* (sensitive). So, before learning a cognate, just check whether is a true or a false one.

▶ **High frequency vocabulary.** If you are taking a well-designed language course, you will be taught words and phrases that are frequently used. If you are studying by yourself, I suggest you use materials with learning activities for high frequency vocabulary, because these will give you the best returns when it comes to communication.

▶ **Frequent collocations.** A smart approach is also to focus on words that are frequently used together. These chunks of language are often called "collocations". Examples of everyday collocations are: *una botella de agua, una botella de vino, un partido de fútbol, un partido político, hablar por teléfono, ganar dinero.* Committing collocations to memory will help you develop more fluency in speaking and writing.

▶ **Expressions for you.** What specific expressions are useful for your current personal or professional situation? Do you remember John from the chapter on motivation? He decided to learn some Spanish phrases related to building construction because he was dealing with Spanish speaking builders. And when he went back to Spain to supervise the building work, he noticed that being able to use some specialist terms in Spanish put him in a stronger position during the negotiation of contracts.

Some **vocabulary rules** can also help the easy transfer of knowledge between languages.

For example:

▶ Most words ending in -ation in English change to *-ación* in Spanish (celebration-*celebración*, classification-*clasificación*).

▶ Many words ending in -ity in English change to -idad in Spanish (fertility-*fertilidad*, ability-*habilidad*).

▶ Adverbs ending in -ly in English change to -mente in Spanish (happily-*felizmente*, simply-*simplemente*).

Two golden keys

Cognitive psychologists have found that **interest** and **understanding** are two of the golden keys for learning. And that makes sense, doesn't it? We pay more attention to and engage more with things that catch our interest, and we remember better what we understand well. I have no doubt about this. I see these principles at work year after year with my Spanish students. For example, when doing revision for the end-of-year exams, the majority of my beginners have no problem remembering the words for food and activities that are popular: *patatas fritas* (French fries), *pastel* (cake), *escuchar música* (to listen to music), *bailar* (to dance), *salir con mis amigos* (to go out with my friends), and *viajar* (to travel).

Three steps to remembering

Now let's imagine that you are in a situation where you want to do intentional study of a set of specific words or phrases in order to memorize them. What can you do? How can you memorize them effectively?

Current research indicates that, in order to retain information in the long-term memory, you need to create multiple connections and engage in spaced practice and spaced recall. Let´s discuss these three steps in more detail.

Creating multiple connections involves associating the form of the Spanish words you are learning with their meaning(s) and with how they are used. It is a creative process because multiple associations can be made with the vocabulary we want to learn. Here are examples of multiple connections that you can make to learn a Spanish word like *queso* (cheese):

▶ Associate the word with a picture of cheese, drawing it on paper or visualizing it.

▶ Listen to how the word *queso* is pronounced, paying careful attention to the sounds and the stress. Notice that *que* is the stressed syllable and that the vowel *u* is silent here. Repeat the word out loud several times.

▶ Write the word in a sentence or a short dialogue which resonates emotionally with you. Doing this is very effective because phrases and dialogues are more meaningful to us than single words. If you like cheese sandwiches, you could write a mini-dialogue such as "¿Qué quiere tomar?" "Un bocadillo de queso, por favor." And then imagine yourself in a café, talking to a waiter and ordering food. Act out the situation in your imagination, making it as real as you can. If you can think of a humorous situation, all the better, because humor causes an endorphin surge and stimulates the frontal lobes, increasing the degree of focus and amount of attention time.

▶ Design a mind map or a set of flashcards with vocabulary related to food and drinks that you would normally order in a café, including the word *queso*.

▶ Color-code. When writing the word *queso*, use the same color that you use regularly for masculine nouns so that it is visually clear that you are learning a masculine noun. Knowing the gender of the noun will help you use correctly noun-adjective agreements such as *queso fresco*, *queso salado*, *queso sabroso*.

Psychologists and neuroscientists have found that, when the connections we make are meaningful to us, we have a better chance of learning new things well. They have also found that, for long-term retention of vocabulary, we need to engage several senses and take as much advantage as possible of our good visual and spatial memory. That is why learning Spanish vocabulary is more effective if you hear how a word is pronounced, write it down, say it out loud, take advantage of color-coding, and associate the new word with pictures or graphics.

There are many techniques that can be used for creating multiple connections. You could write vocabulary on sticky notes, keep a notebook, design flashcards, use mnemonics, build a "memory palace", and so on. My suggestion is that you pick one or two techniques that you find appealing, try them out for a month or so, and see how it goes.

Once you have created multiple connections, it is time for **spaced practice**. Spaced practice simply means that, instead of cramming, you spread the reviewing of vocabulary over a period of time.

At some points during your spaced practice, you need to test what vocabulary you can and cannot recall without looking at your flashcards, mind map, or notes: this is what we call **spaced recall**. Researchers have found that going through the process of trying to remember without any cues is essential for strengthening our memory of what we are learning.

Spaced recall can be a collaborative activity. You can test yourself or ask somebody to test you. Many of us will remember from our schooldays when a friend or family member would ask us questions about the topics that we were preparing for an exam. If you do ask somebody to test you, remember to choose someone who is positive and reasonably demanding so that you neither get discouraged nor get away without doing the work you need to do. As in so many other areas of life, it is a question of finding a good balance!

Acknowledging and celebrating our progress is a smart thing to do – although not easy for most of us because we have not been encouraged to celebrate progress during our education. Yet we do thrive on positive reinforcement: it makes us happier and energizes us to carry on learning.

So, how are you learning vocabulary? Are you combining learning by exposure with intentional learning? Have you ever practiced the three-step approach of intentional learning that I mentioned? If not, are you willing to experiment with it?

10 ▶ Strategies for pronunciation

Achieving a good basic level of pronunciation in standard Spanish is simple for most students, first and foremost because most single Spanish sounds correspond with a single letter of the alphabet. That means that it is possible to easily predict the pronunciation of words you read and to transcribe new words you hear. Two further advantages of the language are that you only deal with five vowel sounds (a, e, i, o, u), which are pronounced the same every time you come across them, and that word stress rules can be summarized in just three statements.

For these reasons, most students of Spanish develop a good basic level of pronunciation fairly easily. The challenge is obviously greater for students whose mother tongue does not have some of the Spanish sounds. Achieving good pronunciation requires more intense, focused practice for these students.

Listen and repeat activities

Over the years, I have seen many students from all over the world improve their Spanish speaking skills considerably in a short period of time by using the listen and repeat strategies I am about to discuss. The strategies are suitable for everyone, and only require the use of Spanish audios or videos with transcripts. Ideally, the topics and language of the audios and videos should be interesting and useful for you. It is also a good idea to make sure you understand the vocabulary that will come up before starting the pronunciation practice, otherwise your mind will be busy trying to work out the meaning of words while you practice. You will start thinking, "What does 'x' mean?" Your attention will be divided, and you will lose the focus on the pronunciation work.

Transcripts are helpful for some of the steps of these practices because connecting spoken language with the written form strengthens long-term retention. Having said that, it is important that you have periods of practice without the transcript and devote your full attention to the sounds. Both practices are complementary.

Listen and repeat ladder ONE

1 ▶ Listen to the audio. Just listen. Listen to the sounds. Enjoy it. You are building a memory of the sounds of the language, and that is the basis of good pronunciation.

2 ▶ Listen to and read chunks of the transcript. Listen first in silence, then pause and repeat the chunks out loud. For example: a) listen and read in silence "¿Dónde vives?", b) press pause, c) repeat the chunk of language out loud as well as you can.

3 ▶ Do intense and focused practice on challenging words. But do not get obsessed, otherwise the practice becomes counterproductive. Notice how, as you keep repeating, the reproduction of sounds becomes easier and more natural. Acknowledge your progress. Keep the experience positive. Enjoy it.

Then go through the same three steps without using the transcript.

Listen and repeat ladder TWO

1 ▶ Practice speech shadowing. Play an audio or video and repeat what is being said immediately after the speaker. Follow the speech very closely, and repeat as if you were the speaker's "shadow", reading the transcript if necessary. No chunking, pausing, or drills here. You are doing your best to follow a little behind the pace of the speaker's voice. Once you are fairly comfortable with your speech shadowing pace, it is time to move on to the next step.

2 ▶ Practice speech synchronization. Now it is about your voice becoming one with the speaker's voice, synchronizing with him or her, supported by the transcript. Do your best. Let go of perfectionism. Have fun with it.

3 ▶ Record yourself. Get a voice recorder and the transcript you have been practicing with. Read the

text out loud, record it, and listen to yourself. Enjoy the improvements and notice the sounds or words that may need further practice. Be patient. Remember that developing good pronunciation is an ongoing process.

Listen and sing

You can use similar ladders with listen and sing strategies for Spanish songs. In fact, if you think about it, we often unconsciously take similar steps when we listen to songs in foreign languages. We normally first just listen, then sing along with short phrases, shadowing and synchronizing with the singer, and at some point we sing the song by ourselves.

Listen and sing is a fun and effective informal language learning practice, and easy to set up. Are you ready to create a playlist with your favorite Spanish songs for listening and singing practice? There are some readymade playlists on my YouTube channel.

More pronunciation tips

A ▶ Start simple, start with words. Get into the habit of familiarizing yourself with the pronunciation when checking new words in the dictionary. Click on the audio icon of your online or app dictionary, and listen and repeat. Do a few drills on the spot. It pays off. By doing this, you are building your speaking and listening skills step by step.

Let's look at an example of the practice you could do while you listen to the pronunciation of a word like *particularmente* in your online dictionary:

1 ▶ Listen for and identify the stressed syllable: *particularMENte*.

2 ▶ Break the word into chunks (*parti-cular-MENte*) and pronounce each chunk separately. Words that initially look daunting to pronounce become manageable if you simply start by breaking them down and pronouncing the chunks one at a time.

3 ▶ Make the chunks progressively longer and say them out loud until you are able to pronounce the entire word without pausing: *parti-cular-MENte > particular-MENte > particularMENte*. Now listen again to the audio. Are you getting closer to the dictionary pronunciation?

If you still struggle to pronounce the word, it may be because:

▶ you have not listened enough to how it sounds, so you actually do not have a good memory of the sounds and stressed syllable. More listening repetitions are needed.

▶ the word contains sounds that are still challenging for you to pronounce. Patience is needed here. You may need to accept that reproducing those sounds is going to require more time and practice.

▶ your focus is not good. Your mind is wandering, busy thinking about other things. Can you bring your full attention to the pronunciation practice activity?

B ▶ Learn three basic rules of word stress. These three rules show you how to identify the stressed syllable in all new words you encounter:

1 ▶ Most Spanish words are stressed on the penultimate syllable. These words end in -n, -s, or a vowel (a, e, i, o, u), for example: CaRAcas, *eXAmen*, *aMIgo, cerVEza, FIESta.*

2 ▶ Other words (ending in consonants other than -n and -s) are usually stressed on the last syllable, for example: MaDRID, *espaÑOL, amisTAD.*

3 ▶ If a word does not follow the rules above, the stressed syllable will be shown with a written accent, for example: *autoBÚS, inGLÉS, teLÉfono, MÚsica.*

C ▶ Get pronunciation software. If you need to do intensive work with specific sounds of Spanish, I suggest you buy multimedia pronunciation software that shows how to position the speech organs and provides a variety of multimedia activities for practice. Pronunciation software is worth the investment for the majority of students, and particularly necessary for those who find that using listen and repeat strategies is not enough to get them to a good basic level of pronunciation.

11 ▶ Are you enthusiastic about grammar?

"How many of you are looking forward to learning how to speak good Spanish?" I often ask my students at the beginning of a course. Their response is predictable: the entire class, looking rather happy, raise their hands without hesitation. And when I ask, "How many of you are looking forward to learning Spanish grammar?" the response is also rather predictable: about three out of 18 students raise their hands without hesitation. Later on, when discussing the reasons behind their lack of enthusiasm, students tell me that grammar is:

▶ hard to understand
▶ hard to memorize
▶ not important for speaking.

I can easily empathize with their comments. I used to feel the same when I was at school, and even during my studies at university. Although I enjoyed studying Spanish grammar up to secondary education, I remember finding it a rather difficult and boring subject at baccalaureate level. I could not understand the purpose of analyzing in so much detail all the complex grammar structures we were taught. "What do I need this for?" I wondered many times.

Fortunately, many current foreign language courses have a communicative approach to the teaching of grammar. The emphasis is on teaching students the grammar needed for real-life communication. For example, let's imagine that you are on a beginners' course and learning how to talk about your weekly routine – activities that you normally do during the week. If the teacher uses a communicative approach, she will teach grammar points that will enable you to talk about your routine activities in real-life conversations: for example, reflexive verbs (*levantarse*-to get up, *ducharse*-to have a shower, *acostarse*-to go to bed), and periphrasis (*tener que* + infinitive-to have to do something). Current communicative teaching approaches spare students long theoretical explanations and instead focus on the structures used in everyday communication. This pragmatic approach to the teaching of grammar has been a major improvement in foreign language teaching. I hope you get to experience it.

If you are one of those students who, for whatever reason, has a resistance to studying grammar, do remember that learning key Spanish grammar rules and structures will improve your communication skills in three ways:

▶ You will be able to **communicate with more precision.** As you probably know, different Spanish verb endings convey different meanings. So saying, "Trabajo en la universidad" is not the same as saying, "Trabaja en la universidad." In the first sentence I am saying that I work at the university, while in the second sentence I am saying that he or she works at the university.

▶ You will be able to **use the language more creatively.** For example, if you are able to use a variety tenses, you can understand and talk about past, present, and future actions and events in conversations. You cannot do that if you can only handle the present tense.

▶ You will **develop more fluency** in speaking and writing. Once you have understood and automatized word order, agreements, verb endings, and so on, you will not need to pause so much to think about how to say what you want to say: you will not hesitate so much.

Please note that I am not suggesting that you need to have perfect grammar to communicate in Spanish. No. Perfection is neither necessary nor possible. Errors are a natural part of the process of learning, and the truth is that, in many cases, we are still able to understand and communicate essential information with less than perfect Spanish grammar. But it is also worth keeping in mind that a good command of basic grammar will enable you to be more precise, creative, and fluent in Spanish.

In the medium and long term, a command of basic grammar pays off. It is worth the effort.

12 ▶ Automatizing grammar

What areas of Spanish grammar are you going to focus on? Have you thought about this question? Because, as with vocabulary, some grammar topics are more critical than others for good communication. For example, I would say that frequently used Spanish verbs deserve your full attention. I would recommend that you learn well how to form the verbs and verb endings. Focusing on the grammar of verbs is especially important if you want to be good at speaking the language, since a verb occurs in nearly every utterance and conveys three types of critical information: the action/feeling/thought, who or what does the action, and when.

Another aspect of grammar worth focusing on is rules that have few or no exceptions. One example is the Spanish grammar rule on word agreements: articles and adjectives agree with the noun they describe in gender and number. Understanding and memorizing this statement is smart because you will need to use word agreements constantly when communicating in Spanish.

Fortunately, most self-study courses and Spanish grammar learning materials contain summaries of grammar points frequently used in everyday communication. The summaries will be useful in giving you guidance on what to study.

A multidimensional strategy

It is worth remembering that knowing the verb endings and grammar rules of a foreign language by heart does not automatically translate into being able to use that knowledge easily when speaking or writing. Actually, it can be rather frustrating to experience how, in spite of knowing the rules, we are unable to apply them fluently in communication. When there is a mismatch between knowing and using the rules, it means that we have not automatized their use yet.

The solution to automatizing grammar is to take a multidimensional approach. For example, let's imagine that you want to be able to use the preterite and imperfect tenses. A multidimensional approach for automatizing the use of these two tenses would involve combining formal and informal learning activities such as:

► getting **extensive and intensive exposure** to the use of the two tenses through interesting and comprehensible reading texts and listening materials. Biographies are excellent materials for this purpose because describing what people have done in their lives requires the use of both past tenses. And, in addition to being exposed to many examples of the preterite and imperfect, you learn about the lives of interesting people.

► using flashcards or another technique that helps you to intentionally study and memorize the form of the tenses.

▶ doing classic grammar drills with activities from your Spanish workbook or software.

▶ doing written and speaking activities that require you to use both tenses, for example: discussing past holidays or attendance at cultural events, talking about changes you have experienced since you moved to a new job or new place to live, discussing things you used to do when you were younger, and so on.

▶ asking for constructive feedback from a teacher on your progress in using the two past tenses.

▶ listening and singing along to songs with lyrics containing the preterite and imperfect tenses.

13 ▶ Flashcards

I was marking Iwona's essays and, as on previous occasions, I was impressed by the wide range of vocabulary she had used. Her essays were amongst the best I had seen in all the years I had been teaching Spanish. "What do you do to produce so much good vocabulary, Iwona?" I asked her when returning her essay.

"Oh, I use flashcards cards," she replied.

"How? What kind of flashcards?"

"I make flashcards of the vocabulary I want to learn after each Spanish lesson. Then I revise them twice before I go to the next lesson. I usually revise on Wednesdays and Thursdays while I'm at the till of the gift shop where I work. Those days are quiet – there are times when there's nobody around. I spend about ten minutes reviewing the cards – it takes very little time. I do it because I don't like checking the dictionary constantly when I'm writing. I prefer to write when I already know the vocabulary."

Felicity was attending the same Spanish class as Iwona, but she was struggling with the course. Although she was a very motivated student, one of the most motivated in her class, Spanish was a rather challenging subject for her. I was not surprised about that. She had just arrived in the UK from a very small town in a faraway country to study a demanding university degree course with only a basic level of English. On top of all that, she had to work an average of 20 hours a week to pay for her living expenses. No wonder she often looked exhausted in class.

The day of the speaking exam was getting close, and we were about to start doing revision. Felicity was looking unusually confident as she walked through the door that day. And I was impressed by her speaking performance during the class – it was the best speaking I had heard from her since the beginning of the year. When I asked how she had managed to catch up so much and so well, she smiled, pulled out a stack of bright yellow and green flashcards from her bag, and spread them on the table. I could see that the cards had been nicely crafted with careful handwriting and small sketches. She went on to explain how she had decided to try flashcards after our class discussion on language learning strategies. "It was so easy and so much fun to do revision with the cards, Maria! It was fun making the cards, too," she said.

The stories of Iwona and Felicity are just two examples of the many positive experiences that my students have had using flashcards. They find the cards useful for regular study and exam revision, and I notice many, in some cases impressive, improvements in both their performance in Spanish and their self-confidence.

Designing flashcards

There are many different ways of designing flashcards. Take a creative approach: you can play with the content, format, and illustrations. For example, you could use flashcards for learning words, collocations, questions and answers, rules, grammar structures, or short lists of verb endings. And you have a choice of making paper flashcards or using software. Some **flashcard applications** are very convenient for foreign language learning: they include audios, voice recorder, vocabulary games, and a spaced repetition system. But although these kinds of applications are very popular, I still find students who prefer using **paper flashcards**, or who prefer combining both formats, electronic and paper.

Regardless of the type of content and format you use, I recommend you explore the application of four simple principles that have been found effective for long-term retention of information:

▶ Add relevant **images and symbols.** There is evidence from research studies that we remember information much more easily when it is supported by visuals.

▶ Use **color-coding** systematically. For example: stick to using one color for feminine nouns and a different color for masculine nouns; and highlight irregularities in verb conjugations.

I am very fond of color-coding: it requires little effort and can give big returns in a language like Spanish. I discovered its power many years ago when I introduced color-coding systematically in my PowerPoint Spanish grammar presentations. After doing that, I noticed that my students used verbs and word agreements with more accuracy, and the percentage of errors in agreements came down dramatically in the speaking test. It was remarkable.

▶ Use different **letter sizes.** The rationale for using different letter sizes is the same as for using color-coding: it directs our attention to differences and helps to establish contrast. Attention to contrast is particularly useful when learning Spanish verbs. If you write the verb endings in capital letters and the roots in lower case, you are signaling at first glance the contrast between both parts of the verb, and reinforcing the message that the main focus of your study is on the endings.

For example:

habl-O
habl-AS
habl-A
habl-AMOS
habl-ÁIS
habl-AN

▶ Group the cards under **topics.** Grouping language under topics such as free time activities, social media issues, job application, and so on enhances comprehension and memorization of the material.

Once your flashcards are ready, you simply need to apply the spaced and recall practices discussed in Chapter 8.

Have you ever used revision flashcards in electronic or paper format? Are you willing to try them out? What content are you going to include in the cards?

14 ▶ A materials kit

Using good Spanish learning materials is very important for making progress with the language, especially if you are not living in a place where you get to hear, read, speak, and write Spanish regularly.

Broadly speaking, I recommend that you build your own materials kit with two types of materials: educational and authentic.

Educational

Educational materials are specifically designed for learning purposes and are great for understanding the intricacies of the language in depth as well as for doing focused practice. The basic kit that I recommend to my students includes:

▶ a self-study course. This would be one of my top priorities because a course, particularly a multimedia course, is an excellent resource for creating the "backbone" of the language.

▶ dictionaries. Both online or app format are helpful, not only because they are convenient to use but also because they enable you to hear how words are pronounced.

▶ a grammar book, software or application. Whichever format you choose, it is important that it gives you clear theoretical grammar explanations, examples of usage, and plenty of grammar activities.

▶ a vocabulary builder. This is not a priority if you are already using a self-study course that deals in depth with vocabulary, but otherwise I recommend you get one.

▶ graded readers. These are excellent resources for "flooding" your brain with Spanish input which is interesting and comprehensible. Have you used them?

Authentic

Authentic materials are a perfect complement to educational resources. They give you the opportunity to listen to and read everyday, up-to-date language produced by native speakers for real-life communication. Other advantages are that there is a wide range to choose from, and most are free and available on the internet. Examples of authentic materials are: information brochures, transport timetables, shop catalogues, comics, cartoons,receipts, announcements, advertisements, newspapers, magazines, books, movies, songs, radio and TV programs, soap operas, songs, children's cartoons, computer games, video clips, tweets, and WhatsApp messages. The list goes on and on.

Are you already using any authentic materials? With such a wide variety to choose from, it should not be difficult to find resources suitable for your language level and interests.

When selecting resources, particularly authentic ones, please keep in mind that you do not need to understand every single word to benefit from them. Having said that, materials should not be overly challenging because, if the language is too hard, you will learn very little and lose confidence. Remember that, as discussed in Chapter 5, the most effective Spanish reading and listening input that you can get should be not only interesting but also comprehensible.

15 ▶ Good courses and teachers

I always recommend people to take good Spanish courses regardless of their level of proficiency – beginner, intermediate, or advanced. A good course provides support with crucial ingredients of language learning such as well-designed topics, a wide range of learning activities and educational materials, and a well-trained teacher. During the lessons, you get many opportunities to focus on, systematically practice, and reflect on language skills (speaking, listening, reading, writing) and different aspects of the language such as vocabulary and grammar. Focused and systematic practice is very important for developing precision in your spoken and written Spanish.

Actually, one of the best things about language courses is that they help in assembling key pieces of the language. In a way, language learning is similar to doing a jigsaw of a large landscape. Completing the landscape gets easier when we start by identifying and assembling together a few pieces of the tree, a few of the river, a few of the mountain, and then, step by step, we enlarge the clusters until the full landscape emerges. A similar process takes place in a Spanish language course: you are helped to identify and put together key elements of vocabulary, pronunciation, and grammar, and to expand those clusters until a big "landscape" of Spanish emerges.

I also recommend people to be proactive in finding good teachers. A good teacher is very important, and by good teacher I mean one who enjoys teaching students, has creative and effective ways of facilitating Spanish language learning, and believes that students can do well when they apply themselves. Good teachers also expect good work, and provide constructive feedback to help students understand in what areas they are making progress and what requires more work and attention. Good teachers make it possible to achieve results that go well beyond what you initially thought possible. It's worth looking for them.

A solid foundation

I opened my inbox and found an email from Jo, a student I had taught the year before.

"Hola María,

Just wondering whether to retake the Spanish beginners' course I did last year or whether to enroll in the next level. Would it be possible to do the beginners' course again? I would like to carry on with Spanish but I know that my basic Spanish is not very good; I would feel more comfortable with starting the year again. What do you think?"

It was nice to hear from Jo again. She had gone through a rough time while taking the course. Although she had a strong motivation to do well, difficult family circumstances led to her missing many lessons and struggling to keep up with her first year at college. I was glad to know that she was back and wanted to carry on studying Spanish.

Jo was willing to retake her beginners' course. Not many people are willing to do that. Retaking is often considered a sign of failure, while speeding forward to higher levels is a social sign of success. But Jo was ready to slow down in order to consolidate a good basic level of Spanish, and I supported her in that because I believe that, in the medium and long term, a solid foundation saves students a lot of time and guards against future stress and struggles. A solid foundation prevents gaps in language knowledge and skills, prevents fossilized errors, and enables students to experience from the start more ease and confidence when communicating in Spanish. That is why, sometimes, retaking a course, particularly at the lower levels, is the smartest thing to do.

What about you? Have you already started learning Spanish? Have you acquired a solid foundation of the language? Or do you need to slow down and consolidate some of the basics before you move on to the next level?

16 ▶ Deep diving

Bob was traveling to Spain for the first time knowing very little Spanish. He was going for a weekend to Barcelona with some friends. They were in adventure mode and had decided not to book hotel rooms in advance. "We'll just go with the flow and look for places to stay once we arrive," he told me before leaving. And so they went.

On his return, I asked about his trip. His face lit up. "We had a great time – loved Barcelona, the food, the night life, the weather. Gaudi's architecture is amazing. We visited the Park Güell, Casa Batlló, la Sagrada Familia. We strolled down the streets of the Barri Gòtic, and we managed to get to an FC Barcelona football match. It's one of the best trips I've ever done! We also made some Spanish friends at the match. I'm planning to go back this summer to see them."

"Did you manage to practice some Spanish?" I asked.

He smiled. "Well, I was surprised how much the basic Spanish we learned in class helped me to make contact with people and get things done. Like the first night, when we went to a café. We were having dinner and watching a football match on the TV, and I started chatting to a Spanish man on the next table. His English was as basic as my Spanish, so we kept talking and switching between both languages. I managed to understand quite a lot of what he was telling me in Spanish and we made a good connection. Later on, he helped us to find accommodation in a hotel nearby.'"

Bob's attitude in class was transformed by his short visit to Barcelona. Before the trip, he had often been distracted in class, more interested in socializing with his classmates than in learning Spanish. But the trip changed him. He paid a lot more attention to the explanations in the lessons and was much happier and more productive in all the class activities. And the transformation showed in his results: by the end of the course, he was doing really well in all the language skills, and he passed his Spanish exams comfortably.

Full immersion in a Spanish speaking country can help you to greatly expand your language repertoire. Daily routine activities such as shopping, ordering food, arranging outings, or talking about your plans with native speakers are ideal situations for intense language practice. For example, a trip to a grocery store easily becomes a lesson on food, instructions, and numbers – you may be reading food labels, asking the shop assistant where to find certain products, reading the product names on your receipt, and hearing the cashier telling you the total of your bill.

This kind of **intense and contextualized** reading, speaking, and listening facilitates smooth acquisition and long-term retention of productive and receptive vocabulary. Receptive vocabulary refers to all the words and phrases you understand when you read or hear them even if you cannot use them when you speak or write. Productive vocabulary refers to all the words and phrases you understand and which you are are also able to produce when you speak and write. Increasing both types of vocabulary is essential for developing good communication skills.

Full immersion also provides many opportunities for improving fluency and enhancing our understanding of cross-cultural values. I remember Paul, one of my Spanish intermediate students, talking about his summer language exchange in Salamanca. He told me how Álvaro, his exchange partner, had often taken him to his family and friends' homes for dinner so that he could mix with native speakers and experience more of the local gastronomy. Paul described those dinners as among the most intense learning experiences of both language and culture that he had ever had.

"Conversations moved swiftly from one topic to another: travel experiences, politics, local gossip, traditions, finances, family plans, and many other topics. It was hard work because, when Spanish people talk in groups, they take turns very fast, but I made an effort to keep up with their turn-taking speed and take part in the conversations. I noticed that my fluency in Spanish improved after the dinners and I got more confident about communicating with native speakers. I also noticed that their family ties are very strong. I lost count of the number of Álvaro's cousins I met and the number of occasions we were invited to stay or eat at his relatives' homes. Even when we went sightseeing to other cities, like Segovia, Álvaro would call them and they would invite us to their home for lunch. I had never experienced anything like that before."

Deep diving into Spanish language and culture transformed Paul's Spanish and expanded his cross-cultural understanding. The same happens to many students who spend a good period of time immersed in a Spanish speaking country.

Have you experienced full immersion? Are you considering doing it? Is there any particular country you feel drawn to visit?

17 ▶ More immersion options

There are a variety of options available which offer different levels of immersion in Spanish language and culture. For example, you can find literally hundreds of online language exchange sites for face-to-face or Skype language exchanges. Some sites integrate access to free and premium multimedia materials with access to online tutors and forums where you can interact with Spanish native speakers. They provide a good virtual environment for meeting and learning Spanish with people who are enthusiastic about foreign languages, traveling, and discovering new cultures. Have you tried any of these sites?

Other smart options are social events organized by Spanish clubs. Online networking sites such as meetup.com are good places to find clubs where Spanish native speakers and students of the language get together and organize exchanges, watch films, discuss books, go salsa dancing, eat out, and so on. When my students attend these types of clubs, they frequently comment on the friendly atmosphere, many end up making friends, and I often notice considerable improvement in their speaking skills and self-confidence.

Last but not least, there are some classic, low cost, and convenient options for immersing yourself in Spanish language and culture: books, music, TV, YouTube, radio programs, and movies. I cannot recommend these highly enough. Nowadays you do not even have to travel anywhere to access a wide range of music, movies, programs, and books – you can get them at reasonable prices or for free on your mobile, tablet, or PC. Access is easier than ever, and having so much choice available means that you are sure to find something that interests you. Once you have the resources, you could do activities such as:

▶ reading for pleasure. Choose stories you like with a level of Spanish comprehensible to you. Read for pleasure, just as you do in your mother tongue or other foreign languages you speak. The language should be slightly above your current level so that it stretches your ability, but not so difficult that you have to constantly check the dictionary – unless, of course, you enjoy doing word by word translations!

▶ listening to songs. Find Spanish songs that you like and just listen to them. Even if you do not understand a lot of the lyrics, you will become familiar with the sounds of the language, and some vocabulary will stick in your mind as you listen. Remember that, to imitate well the sounds of any foreign language, you first need to hear them.

▶ listening and singing. This is an informal and enjoyable way of improving your pronunciation, listening skills, and vocabulary. The association of rhythm and language helps you to remember more easily the chunks of vocabulary that come up.

▶ listening to the radio. This is an ideal activity at higher intermediate and advanced level, and it is simple to set up. There is a wide range of programs on the internet. What do you prefer? Comedy? News? Entertainment? Educational programs? Listen to the programs and you will refine your listening skills and acquire more sophisticated vocabulary for discussing a variety of topics.

▶ going deeper into movies. I guess that you do not need much encouragement to watch movies: this is a classic activity for people who are interested in learning foreign languages. And the great thing is that, besides being pleasurable, watching movies has three other major advantages for language learning. First of all, the characters in the movie show us how to use Spanish in real-life environments: home, workplace, public spaces, and so on. Secondly, studies have found that the association between spoken words and images in audiovisual materials helps us to better understand the meaning of language and store it in our long-term memory. And thirdly, you get to learn a lot about the culture of Spanish speaking countries because the stories contain information and opinions on current affairs, politics, history, art, science, and so on.

A word of caution: use subtitles wisely. There is not much point in watching movies in Spanish if you can hardly understand what is being said. In that case, it is better to turn on the subtitles of your mother tongue or another language you are proficient in. Remember that, in order to learn a foreign language, we need to be able to, first of all, understand it. So only turn off the mother tongue subtitles or use Spanish subtitles once you understand the materials quite well. Then, turning on the Spanish subtitles is a great way to learn new vocabulary because you are listening to words, seeing the context in which they are used, and reading their spelling all at the same time. You are creating multiple connections that lead to a deeper learning of words and phrases.

Some questions before we move on to the next chapter. What are your thoughts on these immersion options? Have you tried any before? Is there any other that you would like to try?

18 ▶ On ceilings

It was Laura's turn to speak. Everyone's attention turned to her.

"My English will never be good," she said resolutely, looking at the workshop leader and the rest of the class.

Fay, the workshop leader, thanked her for sharing and a few minutes later closed the morning session with a summary of the main points we had discussed about self-limiting beliefs.

I was puzzled by Laura's comment. She was not a native speaker but we had been together in group discussions and my impression was that her English was very good. What made her believe that it was not good? I was curious.

At lunchtime I found her sitting by herself.

"Do you really believe that your English will never be good?" I asked.

She gave me a "how-do-you-dare-to-ask-me?" look and continued sipping her juice. No answer.

"I was puzzled by your comment because your English sounds really good to me."

She fixed her eyes on mine and burst out loudly, "Can't you hear it? Can't you hear my foreign accent? I will never get rid of it."

"Yes, I can hear your foreign accent but I can understand you without any problem. Anyway, have you lived in the UK or any English speaking country for a long period of time?"

"No. I have just learned English in school and at university in my country," she said self-righteously.

"Have you taken a pronunciation course?"

"No."

The bell rang. It was time to go back to the training room for the afternoon session.

The workshop teacher welcomed us warmly back into class. She explained that we were about to put into practice some of the theory discussed in the morning session. For the next activity, we would get into groups of four to discuss self-limiting beliefs that we wished to overcome. One person would share, and the other three would listen, ask clarifying questions, and brainstorm suggestions.

We stood up and moved around, slowly forming small groups. I sat next to Jenny, a pleasant and articulate middle-aged woman I had met in the morning. Two other people, Sarah and Tanuj, joined us.

Jenny volunteered to start. She straightened her body in the chair and started with the poise and confidence of someone who is good at public speaking.

"I would like to get rid of the belief that I am not good at learning foreign languages. I was not good at languages at school. My German teacher always said that my grammar was poor. I barely managed to pass the compulsory exams, and then forgot all about learning foreign languages until recently. But my partner and I are planning to take a sabbatical to travel around the world next year, and we'd like to start with a long trip across Latin America. I would love to learn some Spanish before the trip to be able to talk and mix with the locals and to get closer to their culture. My local adult education college runs Spanish evening courses but I keep postponing enrolling. I'm not sure whether I'll do well." Her body language had changed. She no longer looked like a confident woman. Now she looked as fidgety and sad as a disoriented child.

The group began to ask questions.

"What made you think that you weren't good at learning languages when you were at school?" I asked.

"I didn't understand grammar – I found it hard. My teacher also said many times that my grammar was poor. At one point I just gave up on the language and concentrated on passing the exams. I passed with a very low mark."

"What makes you think it will be the same now?" said Tanuj.

"I'm a lot more motivated than I was at school, particularly because of our trip to Latin America, but I haven't learned more grammar since I left school. I'm not sure whether I can do any better now."

After a few more questions and comments from the group, Jenny started looking more relaxed.

The self-development workshop ended a couple of hours later. The sessions had been emotionally intense and insightful, and the stories of Laura and Jenny remained in my head. I could connect very well with their frustration and lack of confidence. I had experienced very similar emotions while learning English as a foreign language. At one point, when I was at intermediate level, I remember thinking that I had reached the ceiling of my capacity. I was convinced that my pronunciation, vocabulary, and grammar were never going to get better. To say that it was frustrating would be an understatement. But somehow I kept going and broke through that ceiling, and some time later I found myself reaching advanced level English.

Fortunately, my motivation to learn was stronger than my fears. I wanted to live and work in the UK and other English speaking environments without experiencing so many limitations when communicating in English. I am fairly talkative when it comes to things that I care about. I could not settle for not being able to engage fully in conversations that mattered to me. Strong motivation was on my side. Also, while teaching and researching the way we learn foreign languages, I came to understand that people who are considered good at languages seem to apply smart learning principles and strategies which can be replicated. This understanding was, and still is, one of the most empowering insights of my education.

Self-doubt and self-limiting beliefs kick in during the process of learning for most of us. They are often rooted in negative reinforcements received in childhood from teachers, family members, or other people in authority, just as in Jenny's case. We end up believing we are not good at grammar, not good at speaking, and so on, and somehow we conclude that this is the truth and will stay like that forever. We carry around those beliefs unconsciously without asking ourselves: Are they really true?

Now I have taught Spanish to more than a thousand students of many nationalities, from beginners' to advanced level, and I have not yet met a student who could not overcome challenges when they had strong motivation and good guidance, and were ready to put in the necessary work. They always succeed. **There is no ceiling.** Remember that.

19 ▶ What to do next?

"A journey of a thousand miles begins with a single step." Lao Tzu

Now you have read the book, are you wondering what to do next to start learning or to improve your Spanish? There are many ways of doing it. One would be to take this simple three-step approach:

Step 1 ▶ Identify your motivation. I highly recommend that you start by identifying what makes you enthusiastic about developing your ability to communicate in Spanish; clarity will make the process more meaningful, and will give you a lot of stamina. So look at the questions in Chapter 1 and clarify what motivates you.

Step 2 ▶ Get focused and energized. Write down your Spanish learning goal(s). You can use the tips for general goal setting in Chapter 4.

Step 3 ▶ Explore and assess. Which particular strategies would support your current Spanish learning goal(s)? Choose one or two strategies that appeal to you and that support your goals, explore them, and see what results you get after a while. For example, if your general goal is to get an official certification in Spanish, your primary strategy could be to enroll in a DELE or SIELE exam preparation course. You could also enhance your self-study skills by using graded readers and flashcards while taking the exam courses.

If your general goal is improving your listening and speaking skills, you could create a song playlist and practice using the listen-and-sing strategies we have discussed. Try them out for a month or so. Notice your improvements. Enjoy the process and the progress you are making, and identify areas that need further language work.

Whichever strategies you use, I hope you will keep in mind the advice given in Chapter 3 about combining formal and informal approaches. Most of us have been so used to studying sitting at a desk that we find it hard to use songs, movies, dancing, and social outings for learning a language. But, as I said before, the combination of both approaches is highly effective.

And this brings us to the end of the book! I hope you have been inspired to take action and explore smart ways for learning Spanish. I wish you a fruitful and enjoyable exploration, and look forward to meeting you in my coaching and training events.

¡Gracias y hasta pronto!

María

@MariaBHermida

20 ▶ Acknowledgements

To my parents, Jorge and Teresa. I am eternally grateful for your love, for giving me access to excellent formal education, and for letting me choose a university degree in Education. It was a wise decision.

To the students and teachers who have attended my lessons, coaching sessions, and workshops throughout the years. Thank you for coming, for your enthusiasm to learn Spanish and discover Hispanic culture, and for your efforts, your questions, and warmth. Special thanks to Elmira, Gwen, Juliet, Lucy, Madalina, and Mariia for your generous collaboration in my last vocabulary learning strategies research project. It has been great working and learning together with all of you.

To my meditation teacher, Ratu Bagus, and our international community. Thank you, thank you, thank you for the love and laughter that have made it possible to achieve so many things that appeared impossible, like finishing this book.

To my mother, Teresa, my brother, Marcos, my uncle Santiago, and my friends: Aida, Antje, Anurago, Belén, Carmen, Cristina, Fiona, Gemma, Huang Dian, Iris, Jose, Kauser, Lili, Lutz, Lynne, María José, Mariam, Miriam, Masha, Nadia, Paloma, Pepe, Rosa C., Rosa G., Rosa M., Renate, Rosina, Stefan, Tjasa, Vijay, and Yuri. Thank you for the cheerful encouragement through the highs and lows of this writing project. In different ways, and at different stages, your love, friendship, and enthusiasm kept me going.

To Anurago, Cristina, Lynne, Nina, and Vijay. Thank you for supporting with your talents and good vibes the editing and designing processes. My stress levels dropped dramatically as soon as I knew I could count on your help. I am very grateful to you.

To the lecturers at the UCL Institute of Education, my colleagues at the University of Westminster, Consejería de Educación en el Reino Unido y República de Irlanda, ELE-UK, Instituto

Cervantes London, Dr. Julio Giménez, and Vijay. Thank you for the many stimulating discussions we have had about language learner education. They have been instrumental in articulating many of the ideas I present in this book.

To researchers in applied linguistics, cognitive psychology, and educational neuroscience. Thank you for the many insights into the process of language learning. Special thanks to Dr. Andrew Cohen, Dr. Anna U. Chamot, and Dr. Rebecca Oxford for their pioneering and inspiring research on language learning strategies.

And thank you to you, reader, for your interest. I hope you now feel better equipped to manage and facilitate your own learning of Spanish. Do not hesitate to get in touch to share your experiences of applying smart strategies, or simply to send feedback on the book. In the meantime, all the best!

21 ▶ About the author

¡Hola! I am the founder of SMART-Learning for Spanish, and a Senior Lecturer at the University of Westminster (London), where I have been coordinating the Spanish Open Language Program and conducting research on language learning strategies since 2002.

At SMART-Learning for Spanish, I design and deliver training and consultancy programs for students and teachers on smart ways of learning Spanish as a Foreign Language. The training helps students to take effective control of their language learning process, enjoy it more, and experience increased confidence and motivation for learning the language.

I conduct teacher trainer workshops at the Instituto Cervantes London, and have delivered talks and teacher training on language learning strategies for institutions such as the University of Westminster, Universidad de Salamanca (Spain), Consejería de Educación en el Reino Unido y República de Irlanda, University of Nottingham

(UK), and Instituto Cervantes (London). I am also an examiner for Cambridge International Examinations.

My approach is based on more than 20 years' experience of teaching Spanish as a Foreign Language, and incorporates research from the fields of applied linguistics and cognitive psychology.

I have worked in British and Spanish educational institutions, teaching Spanish for General Purposes and for Business, and I have coached students for exams. I also have extensive experience as an examiner, course developer, and learning advisor.

I gained my BA (Hons) in Education at the Universidad Pontificia de Salamanca (Spain), and later completed an MA in Modern Languages in Education at the University College of London Institute of Education. I have been trained in "Improving Language Learning Styles-and-Strategies-Based Instruction" at the University of Minnesota (USA), and in coaching skills at the

University of Westminster and The Coaching Academy. I hold a Certificate in Spanish Language Teaching to Adults from International House Madrid and a EUROLTA Teacher Trainer qualification. I am a Fellow of the Higher Education Academy in the UK.

22 ▶ Resources

Please go to www.smartlearningforspanish.com for:

▶ individual and group coaching

▶ teacher training

▶ interactive talks

▶ materials for learning Spanish

▶ bibliography for research on language learning strategies

▶ links to my social media channels.

Made in the USA
Middletown, DE
04 September 2017